For my family, I'm so glad our stories are interconnected.

Acknowledgements

Tiffany Enns - I appreciated your patience in this process. Your keen mind and consistency make my work better. Thrilled to have you on the team!

Sonja Kolstad - Your fierce feedback has been so welcome and this project is 1000% better because of it. Thank you!

Tim Grahl - Seven years of weekly conversations about business and "What's next?" have been amazing. Here's to 70 more!

Josh Kaufman - You've consistently been a great voice of encouragement. I'm not sure this would've happened without you. Thank you for your expertise.

Derek Kolstad, Marc Ritzema, Brent Gudgel and Dave Mahanes - Thank you for your willingness to talk story principles, screenwriting devices and for being generally awesome people.

Jenelle D'Allessandro - Without your input this project would've been shaped for the worse. Thanks for keeping me on point with this project.

Robert McKee - Your book started this process of thinking differently about story and your workshop solidified it. Thank you for showing where the road leads and how the storyteller never arrives.

Idea Campers - I love our tribe and the sharing and the joy of getting together often. Without you, my Southern California experience would look very different. I'm so thankful for you.

The Out:Think Group Team - You're brilliant, stylish and a great combination of brawn and brains.

Dan Portnoy

THE NON-PROFIT
NARRATIVE
HOW TELLING STORIES CAN CHANGE THE WORLD

Table of Contents

Introduction

INTRODUCTION

> "The world is indeed full of peril and in it there are many dark places. But still there is much that is fair. And though in all lands, love is now mingled with grief, it still grows, perhaps, the greater."
>
> - J.R.R. Tolkien, *The Lord of the Rings*

"We're in a rough spot."

I hear that phrase over and over as I talk with clients. The landscape of philantharopy and communication has transitioned at a rate so fast some organizations are still feeling whiplash.

Senior Staff and Boards of Directors ask questions like: Is this economy going to get any better? When does growth happen again?

Will our budget/giving ever be like it was?

Truth is, I don't see an adjustment anytime soon. (That's the bad news.) Now is the time for creativity, ingenuity and a little bit of risk. (That's the good news.) By far the most risky action in this climate is to bury your head in the sand and try and ignore it.

As traditional giving rapidly declines, new faster, leaner non-profits are springing up everywhere. They engage, they show momentum and it appears they have money left over to start new initiatives.

It would appear that at this time the power shift of organizations that really know how to communicate is being shaken up. Your organization could start competing tomorrow with the biggest non-profits in the country and all you have to do are a few simple things.

It's simple, not easy.

Tell your story and tell it well. Help your audience know your struggles and triumphs in a multi-channel approach with multiple entry points.

Learning to operate in the age of digital communication really isn't shrouded in as much mystery as you might think. Sure, you may not understand everything today, but initiative matters most. In other words, "You just have to begin."

I wrote this book because I know what it takes to communicate a narrative on the web and I believe you can use the same strategies for your own non-profit organization.

My plan over the next several chapters is to give you a framework to help plan your next year by using the metaphor of a Three-Act story structure as a template to help best convey your message.

Again, this framework is simple but it's not easy. Great storytelling is most definitely part art and part science.

Let's get started.

TAKE AWAYS

• At the end of each chapter there will be some takeaways and some next steps about the previous chapter.

• Get a notebook or legal pad and get ready to write down the ideas as they come to you. When working through your story session it's crucial to capture the creative process. I recommend something fresh and don't share it with any other project. Moleskine or Field Notes make some great products for just this type of exercise.

NEXT STEPS

• They'll also be some practical pieces that you can get started on right away.

CHAPTER 1
THE RITUAL OF STORY

What if you could double your online fundraising this next year? Would that much funding change your programming? How about your attitude? Would you be excited to go to work every day?

I'm here to tell you that it's possible.

<u>Your non-profit organization was started to change the world.</u> (Read that again.) You are involved in a mission to change the world and <u>that's</u> a story just about anyone wants to be a part of!

This book is designed to get you to think like the screenwriter of your organization's story. And the best part is: you ALREADY know more than you think about how stories move and shape us. If you've ever been to a movie theater, read a fiction book or told someone what happened over the weekend, you have the tools for engagement.

Where Do We Find Story?

When you start looking for it, you'll find story everywhere. I really believe it's part of human DNA. Stories help us see patterns in our own lives. They help us explain the unexplainable.

The Greeks and the Romans didn't just say, "It's sunny out and then later it's dark outside." They had elaborate, passionate stories of gods and goddesses of action. Their stories told why things happened: Why the sun went up; why it went down; and what was the impetus behind such seemingly mundane things. Even though these myths weren't "correct", to the listener they made life that much easier to comprehend what was happening. These stories also communicated more than causality: they communicated the behavior and the ideals of a culture as well as helped everyday people make sense of their world.

In this book I will teach you how to do the same. Your non-profit's narrative will help explain some of the unexplainable patterns in our culture, and in the lives of your constituents.

Where Do We (Often) Find Story Absent?

Think for a moment and answer these two questions for your own organization:

- Where is story absent from the culture of our organization?

- What kind of story are we telling?

For some insight, look at the behavior of your team. Is there evidence of a scarcity mentality? Or hushed conversations at the water cooler and horribly dry meetings?

I think about this question a lot and started asking people in my workshops for their own answers. I recently posed this question at a workshop and received, what I think, is the best answer: *"Story is most absent from corporate slide presentations."*

Boring Your Audience is a Terrible Thing

Organizations with decent internal communication will have great external communication because it's wrapped in the sheen of marketing. Boring your audience is a terrible thing, and (believe it or not), this begins with how your organization communicates internally.

Think about the last time you were in a grueling meeting filled with buzz words. Did this help or hurt your experience in the meeting? Did that emotion spill over onto your opinion of the person running their meeting or their department?

A boring corporate slide show, when analyzed, actually says a few things. It's not that corporate slide shows aren't telling a story... they are just telling a *bad one*. It's such a bad story that it's probably killing morale. When was the last time you got excited about sitting through a stakeholders meeting with each department sounding off on their recent work? We're missing an opportunity to engage our workplace and create evangelists for our cause.

Storytelling is crucial to survival. You're going to learn how to not only survive as a non-profit organization, but how to change the world with your story.

Are you ready?

Your Organization is On a Hero's Journey

It's been argued that the Hero's Journey is the most common plot ever told. Joseph Campbell first explained this idea in his book, "The Hero of a Thousand Faces", and demonstrated that this plot pervades narratives all throughout history.

The Hero's Journey is a call to adventure and trials. It is a call to transformation and perseverance. It is a call to change the world.

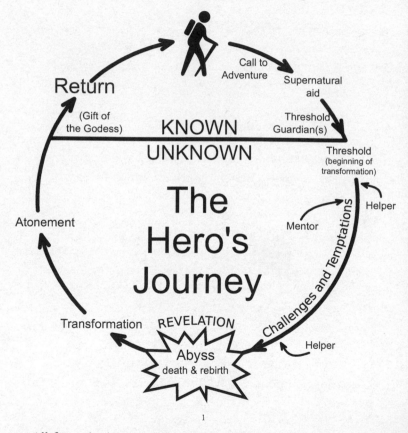

All fairytales have a Hero's Journey. They are all about a central character on a quest.

1 http://en.wikipedia.org/wiki/Monomyth

If I were to tell the story of your life, I'd bet that it could be classified a Hero's Journey. Your organization is on a Hero's Journey, too. You were made to change the world. It's time to push forward into the brilliance of your narrative.

"Like sand through the hourglass..."

Story resonates with us. Storytelling is a ritual we all participate in, because we long to be known.

Since the beginning of time we've related stories to one another. Every ancient text from Hammurabi to Gilgamesh and even the Lescaux cave paintings show that every village had some ideas to express.

In the recent upheaval throughout the Middle East you'll find story. You'll find that story is so central to our human experience, such a raw part of who we are, that people are willing to sacrifice their lives to make sure that it ends well. They already know the end of the story if there is no action and it's not acceptable. Thousands of miles away, we watched as the masses marched, demonstrated, shouted and rioted at the aristocracy. Their collective voice could not be ignored and we were moved by the stories of individuals who would no longer stand by.

Story drives revolution.

- Story communicates a huge amount of ideas — both obvious and some hidden (subtext).

- Story weaves all of humanity together.

It's time to Unearth that Story.

Story is really about more than just the words and the actions. Story is the muscle and sinew that ties together the skeletal facts - we learn context and unearth hidden meanings. Story is a current so strong that when we hear a great story, we can't compartmentalize it.

You are telling a story every day with your life.

"An unexamined life isn't worth living."

-Socrates (c.470 BC - 399 BC)

Telling stories is a way of examining our lives. It's a means to human survival.

If your organization is barely surviving, I would argue that you've likely lost the ability to unearth or communicate your true story. You've lost the vulnerability needed to take a hard look in the mirror and see the guts of your organization for what it really is.

You are not alone and please understand, I'm not condemning you. There is hope, but you'll have to enter this story to see it.

All fiction stories contain truth and usually show insights into the human condition. In what's contained here, I'm going to ask you to walk with me not as a development officer, marketing professional or fundraising coordinator, but as if you are **the screenwriter of your organization's story.** You know your organization better than I do. It will be your job to translate this allegory into your organization. I'll also share the principles that I've found to be most helpful with the non-profits I've worked with.

The Bare Essentials of Story: Just the Facts, Ma'am?

At its bare essentials, a story is made up of a string of simple facts.

Let's take the facts from an anti-trafficking scenario: A child has been born into a life of poverty. She is forced into labor each day for fifteen hours. The camp was closed down and now the trafficking has ended.

That is a terrible story. Those are just facts.

However, if you find out that this child has a name,

and you learn the scenario in which she grew up,

and the town in which it was set,

and what happened that fateful day when she was first

trapped into trafficking,

and if you learn the horrible details of what her life was like for many years: whether she labored daily in a ninety-eight degree brick kiln, or perhaps in a grimy brothel...

Then... a glimmer of hope, a rescue! What was that like? What was the stream of emotions, the spiritual implications, what were the things she smelled and tasted in her freedom? Who were the people involved in her rescue? How did they get the info this was happening at this time?

Pushing Beyond the Facts is a Basic Human Need

We find the best story when we connect the facts. Why? Because we want to understand humanity. It's a basic human desire that we want to understand our world.

²| How can you push beyond the facts? Tell me this: What's one
•| small truth of your organization? *Start there. What are others?*

Are you fighting cancer or building a better life for those affected by this condition? Are you providing clean water to a village that has never had it, or are you giving vision to multiple generations to strive for something they've never achieved before? Is your organization providing a night of shelter for a recently evicted family or are you providing the tools for life transformation?

This truth needs to be explored. Grab your senior team and start brainstorming ideas. I bet there are no less than 15-20 truths about your organization from which you could build a worthwhile campaign.

Prepare for Impact

The best part about the ritual of story is the impact that can happen from the process of telling and listening.

The telling and listening happens every day of every week. Think about it in your own life. You're catching up with people. What's happening? What's going on? Are you okay? We want to hear the story and in turn, we want to tell ours.

Think about family gatherings, they are always laced with story. There's something familiar about hearing certain stories. They remind us that we are connected. They tell us where we started.

"Grannie, tell us that story again about how you and Pop met and fell in love."

Stories give us hope that things can change. They breathe fresh perspective into our lungs and they help us understand the people who are telling it.

This is why it is so important for organizations to ensure that they are effectively communicating THEIR story.

You Know Far More About Storytelling Than You Think.

You know more about telling stories than you realize. For example: It's currently the summer, and I live in Los Angeles. This is a city built on story. Right now the whole area is buzzing with the next big movie. Theaters across America are packed. Millions and billions of dollars are spread worldwide because we want to hear a story. If you've ever enjoyed a film, you know more than you think about storytelling.

Even more, you interact with stories constantly throughout your day.

Think about it. What was the best story you heard this week? Did you overhear a good story at the office Monday morning? Did it involve a birth, a wedding, a divorce, a death?

Next up we need to get some information on you. What are your favorite novels? What captures your attention? This tells me about you, it gives me a window into your preferences. What do you prefer: gritty crime drama or psychological thriller? This helps me know more about you and if I frame a story in the way that you like to hear it, you'll respond.

Let's think about the difference between good stories and <u>amazing</u> stories. What are the stories that we all love? We don't mind hearing the same story more than once. Campbell would argue that we love hearing the same story over and over throughout our whole lives.

Case in point: When "Avatar" came out, it was a blockbuster success. Yet some of us kept noticing that really, we'd seen this story before. We'd seen it when it was "Dances with Wolves." And we'd seen it when it was "The Last Samurai." And we'd seen it when it was called, "Fern Gully." But that didn't stop "Avatar" from making a billion dollars. Why is that? Because that story is the story that we love to see over and over and over again. This is Campbell's "monomyth". In the hands of a master storyteller, they don't have to work hard for us to open our wallets for an experience.

That's the ritual of story.

The Sad Reality: If You're Telling a Terrible Story, No One Cares

There's a phenomenal difference between good stories and great stories. Think about your organization. The story you're communicating is probably self-described as "OK". There are some donations coming in and you're probably surviving.

If your organization has a website, and no one is interacting or engaging with you…I can tell you (with some certainty) that this is because your story is not very good or at the very least - the story you're telling on the web is not compelling.

Good Story vs. Bad Story

Non-profit organizations weren't started to consistently ask for money and talk about the troubles of keeping the lights on. Remember, they were started to change the world. This is the story you need to be telling. Tell me about what is catalytic. Tell me about what brings people together. Rattle the saber.

Right now, think about organizations that you like, the ones that are compelling. Who is telling great stories? Not just good ones, but great ones. That organization that consistently can do no wrong. They put information out about what they're doing, who they are, and who they're helping. The response is consistently off the charts. Whether their website is getting lots of traffic, or their Facebook fan page is overflowing with comments, or their YouTube views are rocketing to the atmosphere, they are set up to literally change the world.

Why is that? Because they are telling a great story.

Think about it, as you watch the media that they've created, and read their copy, it's easy to get caught up in the emotion of what they're doing. You want to be part of it, and so do I. Why? Because it does something to us, it gives us vision and connects us.

These are the kind of story tenants that we need to replicate.

And that's what this book is about.

Let's take a look at some examples of businesses that effectively built their story through the web.

Principle #1: Let's Build a Story that is True

Exhibit A: Domino's Pizza. This is a great story. Domino's decided to launch a new ad campaign because they caught on that customers were complaining about quality. Customers were basically saying, "We don't like this pizza much, it's kind of cruddy cardboard and the sauce is bad."

So what did Domino's start to do?

They said, "We can use this, because <u>this is really our key issue.</u>" And they were spot on.

They put together a campaign based on the fact that they were changing things, that they were investing, and their CEO knew that they had disappointed their customers!

In those commercials and in that ad campaign we saw the truth about Domino's - the truth that they were getting a lot of negative feedback (something we knew) and that they weren't happy about it (something we didn't know). What would've happened if they made promises to make drastic changes and then didn't follow through? We would have written Domino's off because they had our attention with truths, but the story they told was a lie.

Principle #2: Let's Build a Story that Resonates

During the Super Bowl every year we watch "the Super Bowl of commercials." You may not have noticed, but the best Super Bowl commercials build on a truth. Amazingly, sometimes the truths advertised aren't related to the product.

Exhibit B: In 2011, the clear winner in the Super Bowl commercials was the 30-second Volkswagen commercial with the eight year-old dressed as Darth Vader. The commercial is called "The Force."

The truth in this story was this: Kids have great imaginations.

Kids are running around the house in the midst of their grand imaginations, living within their own stories. We've all either done it, seen it, or experienced it. This was a truth of humanity that Volkswagen tapped into.

The actual product benefit that they showed was Dad coming home and activating the remote start with his new 2011 Passat.

The product wasn't the story! Instead, the story said, "Volkswagen knows that you get curveballs everyday, and the Passat will help create special times."

When Volkswagen released the commercial it went viral. Why? Because it was really well done and we connected with the truth of it. Simply put, their narrative resonated with us.

When we're building our story, we have to build on truth and it must resonate with your audience.

Build your story and make sure it reflects your organization.

Principle #3: Keep the Cookies on the Bottom Shelf

Think through the broad strokes of your organization's story for a moment. Where are the points in your story that people can get involved? What resonates easily with your audience? This is the "cookies on the bottom shelf" approach - make it really easy for your audience to interact with you.

Of course, we all know that as a non-profit organization, you can easily build on "slacktivism." Slacktivism is what happens when someone clicks "Like" on your Facebook page. That "Like" click doesn't mean that they are getting active in your cause. It just means that they clicked the mouse a couple of times. "Slacktivism" can deliver an opportunity, if the story is great.

Next up, we're going to go beyond the "broad strokes" and take a look at the fine details of your story. Every story has a structure that is much like its skeleton. Let's build on that skeleton.

TAKE AWAYS

• Think of your communication in terms of telling a larger story.

• You know more about storytelling than you think.

NEXT STEPS

• How is story present in your world?

• How well are you communicating your story?

• Look at the Hero's Journey diagram - how does this compare to your organization?

• What truth can you build a campaign around?

• Think about 2-5 non-profits that are communicating well. Do a quick audit to find out where they are active online and sign up for their email lists.

• How are you communicating story through your website?

• Ask your team how well you're communicating internally.

• Are your communications filled only with facts?

CHAPTER 2
BUILDING YOUR STORY
PART 1 - THEORY

"Get busy living, or get busy dying."

- Andy Dufresne, from The Shawshank Redemption

Your story must be built with boldness but also with care. We need two parts courage and one part artistry. I truly believe that you have it within your organization to make it happen.

When I'm in the initial meeting with a non-profit client, one of the first questions I ask is:

"What does your organization do? What do you solve?"

I'm usually told a five-minute story (which is good). It's usually heartfelt, and in some cases emotional, as they tell me this story. The passion that these staff have for their cause is commendable. The story is important but, if we're going to communicate this story in the digital age, we need to be more concise.

"Can you tell me what you do in one sentence?"

If you can't, we need to work on that <u>FIRST.</u> Deciding on this sentence is just a shorthand for you and other stakeholders. Don't over think it. I bet a lot of very smart people worked on your mission statement - it's not uncommon to hear of an organization spending a year to refine it. Use your current mission statement for inspiration. It might not be very marketing-friendly but that's what you're here for. How can we make that sentence a great statement for the back of your business card?

It's crucial to tell your story well but it's equally important to show how serious you are about your cause. Since the dawn of the internet age, the world has become flat and keeps getting flatter. Your story has to compete with Coke, Microsoft, the blockbuster movie that releases this weekend and everything else in the entire world. You'll only get a moment to share your info. If you can communicate what you accomplish or fight in a sentence, you'll most likely get another moment. Multiple moments and multiple sentences are a paragraph and that's where you can start to flourish in your storytelling.

Another scenario I encounter when talking with a non-profit is the data option. They quote stats and figures to me about their scenario. It's usually well thought-out and succinct and then they say: "This is our story."

Only that's not a story at all; it's the start of a story. As I referenced in Chapter One, facts are the start but their's more to your story. These are facts or bullet points. This is no different from your evening news. It's not bad; it's just incomplete. Facts are important and crucial for credibility. They're also the first thing to get referenced in any story. For example, take a look at the beginning of

Boil down the Mission statement.

Cinderella:

"Once upon a time, there was a widower who married (fact) a proud and haughty woman (opinion) as his second wife (fact). She had two daughters (fact), who were equally vain (opinion). By his first wife, he'd had a beautiful (opinion), young daughter (fact), who was a girl of unparalleled goodness and sweet temper (opinion). The stepmother and her daughters forced the first daughter to complete all the housework (fact). When the girl had done her work, she sat in the cinders (fact), which caused her to be called "Cinderella" (emphasized opinion). The poor girl bore it patiently, (opinion) but she dared not tell her father, (fact) who would have scolded her, since his wife controlled him entirely (mix of opinion and fact)".

The facts are:

- A widower gets married for a second time

- His new wife has 2 daughters

- He also has a daughter

- The new wife runs the house and has extra duties for the first daughter

Not as exciting, is it?

If you rattled off just those facts, I might know the story that you're trying to convey but you're placing a lot of chance on the audience.

By reducing that paragraph to bullet points I took all the heart out of the story. *Heart is why you got into this game, so don't shoot yourself in the foot right out of the gate.* You're the expert on your story. As part of your audience, I trust that the information you're giving me is correct but I need more than facts to be engaged. Show me how you flourish, give me the details, fill in the blanks. Communicating a story only with news items is like trying to get a sense of what a room looks like by looking through the key hole - opinions, details and flourishing swing the door to a great story open wide.

Some have never thought of their organization as a story needing to be communicated. Often it comes down to a "tyranny of the urgent" scenario. Maybe you've thought, "I've got to write this appeal letter." Or, "We need to put some copy together for that new event." It's easier to rattle off some numbers and when the campaign doesn't work well or the response is limited to blame your audience. I know it sounds crazy, but I've seen many organizations operate this way.

Imagine a non-profit was trying to communicate the story of Cinderella by using only the facts written above. If the audience didn't understand that they're communicating the story of Cinderella, where does the fault lie? Is it the audience because they didn't receive the information the way the non-profit assumed it would be understood - or does the storyteller need to communicate better? I'd vote for the latter.

I know the economy has made it crazy for so many non-profits and I'm confident that you've been doing the best you can with what you've been handed. Let's roll up our sleeves and tell a great story.

Essential Elements of Your Story

What are the pieces to a standard story? The standard story is quite simple (but it's not necessarily easy to communicate). It has a setting, a protagonist and an antagonist. It has an inciting incident. It includes three parts: Act One (beginning), Act Two (middle), and Act Three (end) and the stakes must become greater.

Let's start with your setting.

Your Setting is the Railroad Tracks Your Story Runs On

Simply put, the setting of your story is the physical time and place where your organization finds its context. It is the tracks your story will run on. It gives direction and perspective and context.

Think about what happens in a story like "Shawshank Redemption", for example. This story takes place at the Shawshank State Penitentiary in Maine in 1947.

Now consider the setting of a story like "Amistad" set in the colonial period.

Or what if our story is set in space, like "Star Wars"? Or what if this is a story set in 19th-century England, like "Pride & Prejudice"? The setting provides your audience expectation and context for the rest of the story.

Our setting gives us a frame work. If I were to ask a question of the characters in each of those stories about any issue in current events, I'd get three different answers. Understanding the social morays of the day are important to convey a story. It gives us context.

Your organization's setting isn't where the main headquarters zip code necessarily lives, nor where the CEO lives. Your setting is the physical location of the drama. If you work with human-trafficking, perhaps your setting is in Bangkok or the massage parlor down the street or anywhere there is a drug trade. If you feed hungry children all throughout Sub-saharan Africa, then this is your setting.

Defining Your Hero

Next we have to figure out who our protagonist is. Who is your hero? Or your heroine?

Who are some of your favorite heroes or heroines? I think of Danny Ocean in "Ocean's Eleven", William Wallace in "Braveheart", and Han Solo in "Star Wars". Where would stories like "Terminator" be without Sarah Connor? Or "Aliens" without Lt. Ripley? Or "Pride and Prejudice" without Elizabeth Bennett? Each character is very different from the other, but still similar to each other as a hero/heroine. The protagonist is the character we're rooting for!

Each non-profit that exists today is a multi-protagonist story. The organization is a main character, but each person who works for your organization is also a character in the story.

Why is that, you ask? Have you ever met anyone who agreed to work for a non-profit for the money? They made the decision to lend their heart and mind to the cause because they wanted to change the world! This is a powerful piece to your overall story. Each co-laborer's personal story echoes the organization. They changed their life for this cause and that should be celebrated.

Remember that your non-profit is a multi-protagonist story and you'll have some serious brand equity to push forward and dig deeper.

Also remember that your protagonists need to be likeable characters. They have to be human or show their humanity. The argument of whether or not people want a brand to function as a person or as a corporate entity isn't going anywhere. The truth is non-profits, in general, are given more wiggle room in this area because they are focusing on aiding others.

Great Examples of Multi-Protagonist Stories:

- "Crash"
- The "X-Men" Movies
- "American Graffiti"
- "The Royal Tenenbaums"
- "Revenge of the Nerds"

From a story perspective, the protagonist can only be as deep or emotionally engaging as the antagonist is. This is great news for any non-profit with a daunting task like eradicating hunger or bringing clean water to the world.

Every Story Needs a Villain

What's the issue that you're fighting? What is it that you're stopping? You can re-define your antagonist again and again. Your antagonist could be anything from "the breakdown of family," to "drugs and alcohol," or even "socio-economic barriers."

For example, in the human trafficking space, the antagonist is not just "the madame who runs the brothel", it's an approach to "sex tourism" and the socio-economical climate that finds young women and men trapped. Your organization knows that in places such as Southeast Asia, ladies are looked upon to care for the family, and because they are trapped and tricked with very few options, the cycle continues.

The better that you can nuance and delineate your protagonist and your antagonist, the better your story is going to be.

Great Antagonists on the Page and Screen

- Commodus in "Gladiator"

- The Wicked Witch of the West in "The Wizard of Oz"

- The Sheriff of Nottingham in "Robin Hood"

- Voldemort in the "Harry Potter" series

- Darth Vader in "Star Wars"

- Mr. Potter from "It's a Wonderful Life"

- Count Dracula in "Dracula"

- Cruella deVil in "101 Dalmatians"

Isn't it interesting that some stories are so defined by their antagonists that they are named after them? Think about Dracula. Without the Count, there is no story. The same is true for some non-profits.

Most experts would agree that identifying yourself or organization by a negative is risky. So announcing yourself by emphatically stating with a negative action can be plain crazy! **Not for Sale**, **M.A.D.D.** (Mothers Against Drunk Driving) and **Stop Child Trafficking Now** are a few "crazy" organizations that are "mad as hell and not going to take it anymore".

These organizations have taken the notoriety of their names and identify the issues they're fighting. The actions are a catalyst - we understand the gravity of the antagonists they're fighting.

Antagonists aren't limited to being human (think HAL 9000 from "2001: A Space Odyssey"), because even robots malfunction and aliens invade. Look to define your antagonist multiple different ways.

Next time you watch a movie or serial TV, think about the key ingredient to great storytelling. I believe it's the villain. If our antagonist isn't that tough then it's not much of a story, because there isn't much to overcome. If there's no tension, it's not interesting. So if you're fighting cancer or contaminated water remember: The bigger the obstacle, the more powerful your story can be.

A Practical Example: Drawing Your Villain

Let's say your organization fights against the plight of malaria in Africa. Who are you fighting against? I'd frame it so that your audience understands how your organization faces an onslaught of these "big guns" of adversity.

In other words, your Antagonist could be:

- The mosquitos - they carry the disease, as mini ambassadors of death.

- The socio-economic climate - without proper resources, families aren't living in great conditions so infection/reinfection is a real problem.

- The lack of education - many families don't realize the steps they could be taking to prevent standing water, etc.

- The lack of resources - Malaria nets cost just a few dollars and have the ability to change the trajectory of a person's life.

- After you've defined your setting and your cast of characters, next up is finding out why there's a story.

Inciting Incident = Action!

Inciting Incident: The inciting incident is the moment or plot point in a script that kicks the story into motion. It occurs after the set up or exposition and everything that follows the inciting incident should be a result of the inciting incident. It is where a story really begins. It can also be described as the snowball that becomes an avalanche.

It's that moment in the story where the protagonist's world is turned upside down and he/she must then set about resolving the change in circumstances that the incident has brought about. It is generally a clear and defined moment that is easily identifiable. 2

Great Examples of Inciting Incidents

- "Gladiator" - The murder of Caesar by his own son forces Maximus to make a choice.

- "In the Line of Fire" - Frank goes to an apartment to check on a routine call and discovers a serious threat to the life of the president that he must investigate.

- "Star Wars IV: A New Hope" - R2D2 ends up in the hands of Luke Skywalker.

- "Casablanca" - Ilsa returns to Rick's bar.

- "The King's Speech" - A horrifically embarrassing speech is delivered and Albert decides, with the help of his wife, to overcome his stammer.

- "Harry Potter and the Sorcerer's Stone" - Harry receives a magical letter to announce his acceptance at a school for wizards.

In a standard story format the Inciting Incident is the "Why", and without it we don't have a story.

From this action piece the rest of the story unravels. If you ask the question, "Why is this story happening?" you'll find the Inciting Incident within seconds. In most films and TV this will happen between 4-15 minutes into the story. In Cinderella and most fables, this happens on the first page.

Let's transition back to your organization. If we stick with this allegory, the Inciting Incident is where your organization talks about your "Why." You started working in the non-profit sector to change the world and telling your story is how you do it. Your donors and potential donors want to understand causality and your story helps us understand how your organization fits in this world.

So start with it!

Your <u>Why</u> is more Important than <u>What</u>.

You can tell me <u>What</u> you do, but I need to know <u>Why</u>. That's the piece I can get behind. Understanding your causality is inspiring. Inspiration is contagious.

Communicate <u>What</u> your mission is and you can have an audience. Communicate your <u>Why</u> and you'll have collaborators.

Beginning with <u>Why</u> means that you're clarifying: <u>Why</u> did your organization begin this Hero's Journey? What is the problem your organization has set out to solve?

Why was your organization started? Why is it that people decided to work here? Why have you had success in the past?

Simon Sinek, author of *Start with Why*, has been featured on TED. I'd really encourage you to check out his resources; his book is incredible. Simon talks about many organizations that we all know and love. The thing is, once we know their Why, it's easy to see how it frames their world. Sinek says the Why is the thing that catalyzes great leaders and inspires them and I couldn't agree more.

The <u>Why</u> of your organization is equivalent to the Inciting Incident of a narrative. It moves your audience and it moves your story along.

If you can communicate your <u>Why</u> you can catalyze a lot of people toward action. Tell coworkers and watch their inspiration, tell your donors and watch them roll up their sleeves and open their wallets.

Give me a working <u>Why</u> and you'll see an organization moving in the right direction. Your <u>Why</u> can be a tagline in your emails. Your <u>Why</u> can be said on Twitter in 140 characters or less. Your Why is what your audiences and others can say, "YES, I want to be a part of THAT!"

The Tension is Building

"The suspense is terrible... I hope it'll last."

- Willy Wonka

As you build your story, pay particular attention to the significance of your storyline's tension. When we tell stories, we naturally kick up the tension. Why do horror movies do so well? The tension is almost unbearable. It just keeps multiplying, exponentially. How many times have you watched a movie seeing cops investigate a potential crime scene only to be scared by a cat that jumps out? There's a noise from the basement and the classic shot of a character looking down into the dark basement. They call out, "Is someone down there?"

This is the sort of tension you need your audience to live within as you tell your story. Tension is the element of story-telling you need to communicate well in the midst of your organization's crisis moment. Tension draws the audience into the experience. Will you win? How will you fair against your villain?

Near the end of "Silence of the Lambs," agent Clarice Starling is canvasing homes and has stumbled across the serial killer, Buffalo Bill. As she realizes she's confronting the killer, he cuts the lights so she's in complete darkness. All we see is the blackness and all we can hear is her breathing. The next shot is from the perspective of Buffalo Bill: he's wearing night vision goggles and is moving in complete silence. He's watching Clarice, the danger is close...too close. The scene is terrible and incredible.

Tension of this magnitude wouldn't be in the beginning of a story. It increases because we invest in characters as they encounter opposition and we want to see them succeed. If this same scenario was in the first act it might be creepy but it wouldn't have the level of importance and emotional pull. Emotions are an essential part to a master storyteller's repertoire.

Let's look at some examples of tension from non-profits.

The ASPCA shows tension because there is an urgency in the care of animals. Love 146 shows tension by letting you know of all of the people across the globe that are caught in the crossfire of sex tourism and slave labor. Eden Reforestation Projects shows tension by crafting the elusive character of erosion into their stories - once the soil is gone... it can't be replaced.

The best way a non-profit can build that tension is honesty and transparency. Tension can't be solely a story device, it has to be genuine. If your organization is facing a a tough scenario - communicate it. This draws in your audience. Don't worry if the scenario works out well or not, it's important to convey your humanity because it allows your donors/audience the ability to insert themselves in your shoes. Then they'll be asking the questions, "What would I do?". When this happens your audience is active, they're no longer on the bench. They're rolling up their sleeves to help find a solution.

In Case of Emergency, Break Glass

A quick note about crisis communication: it is **not the same** as crisis as a story device.

Crisis communication shows tension but it's a fickle beast. An organization that is doing their job well **does not** plan to use crisis fundraising as part of their story. Crisis fundraising **should only be used when in a "in-case-of-emergency-break-glass" scenario.** A veritable ace up your sleeve. There are enough ways for a non-profit to get blitzed, flanked or blindsided in a year so it's important that you hold on to that card. It's part of your safety net and should only be used in the most dire of circumstances.

Crisis fundraising is taxing on your staff and your relationships with donors so it's important that you're not continually living in crisis mode. We can take a lesson from The Boy in the story The Boy Who Cried Wolf. The boy prompted crisis scenario after crisis scenario and he was eventually eaten by wolves.

If your organization is on the verge of ending or some other massive financial misfortune, then by all means - break the glass and let your donors, members, constituents know of your situation. The best part about a crisis scenario is that is has an end date. This end date lets your audience know that there's something to strive for and also allows for grace to be given as you're so consistently banging the drum of fundraising. It's the same as when our friends try to win contests that require us to vote once a day for a weekend getaway. We can tolerate it because it only lasts a week and we care about our friends.

I've been a part of several crisis scenarios with non-profits. Success is usually found in these scenarios but please use it sparingly.

Additional Note: After deployed, crisis can't be deployed for some time - so be honest and humble when things go bad and get it all out. You can't go back to this "well" for a good while, otherwise you'll be communicating that you're not trustworthy, incompetent or poorly managed - the fickle side to the beast.

Save the Cat, Show me the Hero

When watching a film with a classic three-act story structure the acts can be defined as:

Act One (called the Set-Up) establishes our characters in their world and the relation they have to each other. There's also some sort of small win. In older movies it would be called a "save the cat" scenario. This term was coined by Blake Snyder who released a bestselling book by the same name. Filmmakers show the audience something simple and positive, like a character saving a cat, so that audience can know, "That's our hero!" The first act also holds our Inciting Incident and gives us the <u>Why</u> of the movie.

Act Two (called the Conflict) is the meat of the story and expands until we hit a crisis. We know at the end of Act Two what that hero is going to have to solve to make everything right.

We know who the Protagonist is and who he's going to have to vanquish. Or we know who she's going to have to fight against. It's all set up. Act Two intentionally sets it up.

Act Three (called the Resolution) the conflict has risen and risen and is solved in our climax.

Here's an example:

"The Matrix"

Inciting Incident - Trinity talks to Cypher on the phone and she references Neo. The call is traced and she is attacked by minions.

Act One - The battle between the Agents and Morpheus and his crew has been going on for some time. Both sides have superhuman powers. There's a traitor in the midst of the resistance. Neo defies the Agents (save the cat). Neo is freed from The Matrix.

Act Two - Neo meets the rest of the crew and learns the actual reality he's in. He starts training (the Jump Program, the woman in the red dress) and we learn about the electro magnetic pulse. Cypher dislikes Neo and meets with Agent Smith. Morpheus announces that he's taking Neo to see The Oracle. Cyphers betrayal begins and Neo learns that Morpheus will sacrifice himself for the team. Deja Vu happens and the agents attack. The resistance starts taking casualties, Morpheus and Agent Smith square off. Cypher separates from the group, calls in and wakes up in the real world. He kills all of the remaining team (Dozer, Tank, Switch & Apoc), taunts Trinity about Neo being "The One" and moves to kill him when he finds out he only wounded Tank and he's back with a vengeance. Neo chooses to go after Morpheus.

Act Three - Smith taunts Morpheus, Neo and Trinity show up at the government building and lay waste to minions. Neo starts to believe in his new skills and we see them as he squares off against an Agent. Morpheus jumps to the getaway chopper and is rescued. The team all mange to exit the Matrix except for Neo who squares off against Agent Smith. Neo wins and moves to find another "exit", Sentinels attack the hovercraft and Neo becomes the messianic "One". Neo beats the agents, the sentinels are destroyed and the movie ends with Neo flying by.

Script breakdowns can help you see how actions are packaged together. This insight can help you as you choose to tell the different parts of your story. There are a lot of resources on story breakdown on the web.

Here's a few:

- ScreenplayHowTo.com
- TheScriptLab.com
- ScreenwritingU.com
- McKeeStory.com

TAKE AWAYS

• You know more about communicating a story than you think.

• Communicating the Why of your organization inspires your audience.

• Weave emotion into your story - it's more than facts!

• The setting gives context to your story.

• Each organization is a multi-protagonist story.

• A villain can be a person, idea or a situation.

• Tension is crucial for good story telling.

• Shy away from crisis until it's dire.

NEXT STEPS

• Communicate your mission in a sentence.

• Get to know the stories of your coworkers, it'll help morale.

• Look to communicate staff stories as part of your overall mission.

• Define your villain well; it makes your story better.

• Define your organization's Why.

CHAPTER 3
BUILDING YOUR STORY
PART 2 - PRACTICALLY

> "The beginning is the most important part of the work."
>
> - Plato, The Republic

In any non-profit, we look at our fiscal year on July 1 and ask, "What are we going to do this year? What's going to happen? What are we going to lay out?"

Start by looking at your DNA. What are the things that make your organization "you"? Look at your events. Maybe you have a Gala, or an Auction, or your normal drive for acquisition. When you add up all of your events and campaigns, you probably have a total of two, three, four, but hopefully no more than five. Wouldn't it be better to do three campaigns really well than to do seven not-so-hot? If you do three audacious things every year, that is a lot. Can you imagine? Just three things! You're beating the bushes and gathering people around just three ideas per year!

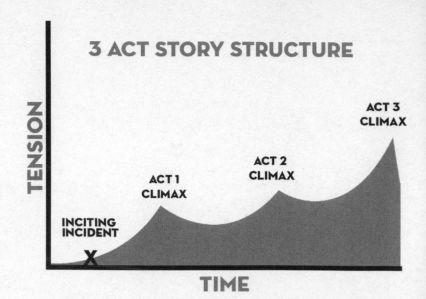

3 ACT STORY STRUCTURE

TENSION

ACT 3
CLIMAX

ACT 2
CLIMAX

ACT 1
CLIMAX

INCITING
INCIDENT
X

TIME

Here's an example of a classic three-act story structure. Please notice that the tension rises as time goes on in any good story. Why is that? Because the stakes keep getting higher!

The same is true as the year progresses for your organization. The stakes keep getting higher, and the tension is rising. This is all part of your story. If there was a flat line across, I can't imagine how terrible that story would be... Actually I think I saw that movie and I walked out.

If we take the diagram and erase the timeline of minutes and replace it with a 12 calendar month - this could be your fundraising campaigns for the year.

We start with your Inciting Incident and then move through Act One into Act Two. Each Act builds on the previous one as tension grows, all leading up to Act Three and its climax.

What do we know about giving in America? Classically speaking, in the Fourth Quarter, we know that the majority of your giving is going to happen - October and November are usually at 8% each and December at 35%. It's not because you're so great; it's because it's just how the world works.

To me, December giving feels like the Third Act climax! The Fourth Quarter is your Third Act!

Consequently, you put a lot of time, energy, and resource into your Third Act. Be as creative as possible. How will you best engage your donors?

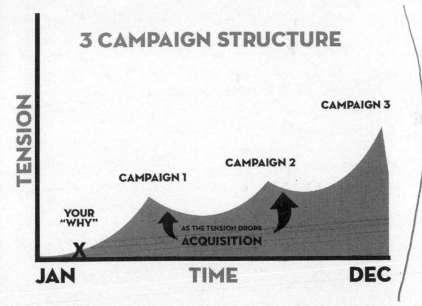

Inciting Incident - State Your <u>Why</u> and State it Well: in January.

Let's look at January, and consider your Inciting Incident. We've talked about your <u>Why</u>. In January, you should <u>State your Why</u>. Say it in no uncertain terms - We exist to: _____. You can create some media around it. Create some videos. Get everything together so you can state your <u>Why</u>. You can do that right now.

What if you spent January and February simply educating your audience? We know from most giving records that giving is usually down in those months. Why fight it and try to come up with the "next big thing"? You'll sink big money into fighting the giving habits of your donors. Instead, let's try to capture their imagination by inspiring them with incredible stories of why your organization exists.

The next step is to <u>state your enemy</u> in no uncertain terms. Extend a purposeful invitation to educate those on the fringes with some new videos (Don't worry, you can use this over and over for your acquisition later in the year). Create a "Your Organization 101" series, or better yet, incorporate it into a welcome series for new signups to your email list. Your welcome series can include video, answers to frequently asked questions and explain why you're fighting this fight. If you want to see what this could look like - sign up for the Portnoy Media email list right now: portnoymediagroup.com/email

How Do You Eat an Elephant? One Bite at a Time.

Most likely the antagonist you've chosen can't be beat in just three months, so it's important that you're showing momentum and progress. An easy way to do that is to get some stories from the people who have been impacted by your organization. Plan on releasing stories at regular intervals throughout the year and release them in different mediums. They don't all have to be short films or mailers. Don't get bogged down in a mode of communication. If your story is strong, it will travel.

Some Ideas:

- A pictorial book of the people most impacted by your cause.

- Blog post with some audio straight from the field.

- Release reports on your impact.

- Show thank you notes from clients.

- Videos of the well being drilled.

- Dossiers showing the prosecution of a child sex trafficker.

These are all social signals that show me, and your audience, how serious you are in getting the job done.

Telling a Good Story Requires Organization Cooperation

So many organizations experience the struggle between Development and Programs. This relationship is symbiotic because without programs you don't have stories to tell, but without money you can't have programming. It's funny to me that so many times non-profits are set up to battle each other internally. It's a classic case of sibling rivalry. If this sounds like your organization, do everything in your power to fix it. You must be one team. You must be one team telling the same story.

Weekly meetings where development gets together with the program side of things is probably the best. The monthly meeting where development pumps program for "stories" is an easy way for resentment to set in. Strong relationships from senior staff and executives are the best way to lead this cooperation.

Make regular deposits in the emotional bank account of your team because things are going to come up and those bonds will be tested. Set up a system or an understanding that will allow for recognition of great work.

For example, set up a special communication between all departments that's for stories only. As they happen this mass email comes around and you can celebrate the great story and your organization's role in it.

Act/Campaign One: February - April *(Campaign One)*

Your Act One climax is likely a campaign that you could do in the spring. In your non-profit's yearly campaigns, your <u>events</u> are often great examples of the Climax of each Act. It is the pinnacle of the action. The climax points of your story are when there's *rescue, hope* and *life transformation.*

Note that this event may not be an actual Gala or Banquet. It might simply be the end-date of your big Matching Grant Campaign, because at this time you find out if you made your goal, or not. In this way, your end-date is *an event!* Make sure that you're campaign has some benchmarks: You're going to raise X amount of dollars by X date. It's so important to be specific.

Equally important is the story behind the story: How are people getting involved? What kind of difference is it making? How has it made a difference in the past? Who is involved?

As Dan & Chip Heath encourage in their book *Switch,* "Find a bright spot and clone it". Show your tribe the best possible response to all of the information you're putting out.

Great Bright Spots:

- The civic group that hears your story and starts a new program to support you.

- The high school class that holds a car wash in your name.

- The business that offers discounts to donors to your cause.

- The film student who creates media showing how she was impacted by your message.

- The donor who organizes a company-wide 5K race with all proceeds going to your organization.

Act/Campaign Two: May - August *(Campaign Two)*

Your Act Two Climax could be your big summer event - the beginning of camp, the food drive or an education summit.

e.g. Summer Push for something specific - 12 new wells, $10 Million for new aftercare homes of trafficking victims or 2,000 new monthly donor partners.

Note: If it is mid-year today and you still haven't stated your <u>Why</u> and stated it well, you should do this right now. Create some media that re-states your <u>Why.</u> You can come back to it in six months. The idea is that you'll use it over and over and over again.

August - September *(As the tension drops - Acquisition!)*

Along the way, don't be discouraged by the feeling of building excitement that rises and falls. It's all part of leveraging the power of your story. This shows humanity. Can you imagine a story where everything always went great? The audience would be bored.

e.g. Social Awareness campaign - "You've helped us this spring with ____Campaign and this summer with ____ Campaign! We're so thankful for you! Would you help us share our work with your network?"

Note: If you're telling a great story, your message is being shared already because you've created a great experience for your donors/audiences. Don't forget to be reiterate your <u>Why</u> to all of your new followers & donors.

Act/Campaign Three: October - December *(Campaign Three - this is for all the marbles!!)*

This is the full court press, pull out all the stops! Retell your story up to this date, help involve your newly acquired audience. They're excited and they'll get involved but you've got to make sure you're connecting them to your needs and the resources you've already created.

e.g. Gift Catalog, Release the media you've created showing your work and the difference it makes. Give people a reason to give. Peer to peer influence, chronicle your volunteers. Be creative!!

Tension: Building throughout and ongoing. The end of the year is coming!

December 26 - December 31 *(This is your last chance for the year. There's automatic tension because of the deadline. As many coaches say, "Leave it all on the field!")*

Note: Increasing the tension, doesn't guarantee that your financial output should increase as well, but it could. The big deal is to make sure that in your largest campaign your organization is functioning on all cylinders, donors are connecting with you the most, that they have the tools they need to help convey your message and that they're telling the best possible story.

January 1 - Reset for your next year. Thank your donors and start to tell your <u>Why</u> all over again.

Exceptions: Your Act One may not begin with the calendar year. Look at where your organization classically brings in the most donations and we'll label that as your Act Three Climax. Then back up your additional campaigns from there. I've worked with some organizations where the summer was their biggest time of activity, So, they launched Campaign One in the fall and they educated their audience thoroughly on the strength of their <u>Why.</u>

Acquisition In a Story Structure

For the non-profit in the digital realm, acquisition can happen all the time. You can do many campaigns when "the tension drops" or in between campaigns. You can talk about the benefits and cite social proof as to why people should get involved in your story.

We talked about tension in Chapter 2 and with tension, set ups need to have a payoff. Again, horror movies do this best. They get you ready, the killer is there (Oh no!), the music starts, and the person walks down the long, dark hallway. Did someone just run by? The tension is rising. Then what happens? A cat jumps out and we exhale. And then we realize, just a breath later, the killer shows up. Why? The payoff has been set up. It's entertaining. It's a great way to convey a story. As you begin your campaigns, there should be goals (set ups) that will be achieved (payoffs). This helps best convey your story and show momentum.

After such tension (set up), there needs to be a report back (payoff). This report back, whether the goal has been reached or not, needs to be communicated. No matter the outcome, it's important to communicate that action was achieved, people were impacted, volunteers thanked for their efforts, and then have the tools available for your audience to tell their networks. This could be as simple as share buttons on your blog posts and as complex as web buttons, specific emails that can be forwarded or personal videos.

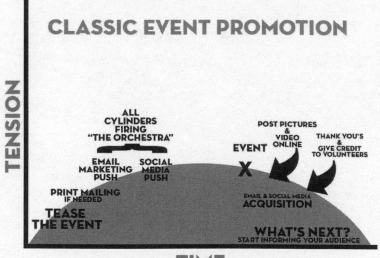

In your organization you have the opportunity to ride the wave of your own story arc. Are you setting up entry-points for your audience to "get drawn in" to your story, even when the tension drops? What will be the big pay off for your audience? Is it an emotional response? Maybe it's the feeling that they are actually, tangibly, fighting the "bad guy" (your Antagonist) along with you?

They are getting co-opted into your story, because you are getting so good at telling it.

Utilizing Events as Part of the Larger Story

The event is not the end! Instead, it's only about 3/4 of the way through your story and your "push." After your event, you need to be posting stories and video, telling the story of the event.

What did people do? What did people think? How was your big <u>Why</u> communicated through this event?

These are easy ways for you to bring your audience along with you.

In the actual campaign you'll follow the same idea. For example, between January to March you'll have a campaign. It's not like the campaign "ends" on March 31st. If the campaign is going three or four months, the next campaign should be "teased" and "foreshadowed" through your first campaign.

Give us Some Previews and Teasers

Audiences love to get a preview of what's going to happen next. Set things up! Give us the inside scoop into what's coming up. Use "Save the Dates" and "pre-announcements." This will make such a big difference.

Now, rewind.

You've got your Inciting Incident, you've set up a whole bunch of media. You've shown us "Your Organization, 101." You've told us everything about you: Who you are, why you're doing these activities, why your staff is set up the way they are; who they are, why they've chosen to be a part of it; what they bring to the table, and what they've sacrificed to get there.

Most importantly, you've communicated the <u>Why</u> of your organization. You've told us why you MUST solve the problem you're setting out to do.

What's next? Tell us about the work you're doing!

Empower Your Audience to Tell Your Story

You're telling the story of what has just happened and how great it was. This is the time to (1) Thank your audience and (2) Ask your audience to <u>tell the story of *their* involvement.</u> (Remember they've just helped you do something incredible!)

Make Sure They Have the Tools to <u>Now Tell Their Friends.</u>

Sadly, so many organizations are not set up for success in this way. They don't give their audience the tools they need to easily talk to others on their behalf.

A few suggestions:

- Create a page that has banners and widgets to convey your campaign on their website/blog, Facebook timeline. This includes videos and blog posts - make sure they are sharable.

- Release some photos of action happening around this

campaign (or video) for your audience to blog and share.

- Ask your audience to send you any videos they may have made while helping you accomplish your campaign.

Once this is done, it's fairly simple. Start all over again with your next campaign. What's the next thing that you're going to do?

Consistency, Authenticity, Consistency

In building your story in the digital age, consistency is power. It's essential that who you are on the web matches who your organization is at events, which matches who you are in print, and who you are on TV. Your message must be consistent.

It means that 1950's rules apply. I wasn't around then but hypothetically speaking, back in the 50's, the duality that we can experience didn't exist. The idea of anonymity that the Internet has brought with it was fine for a time but the social web has changed that idea or mindset. No longer can your organization have a separate public and private face (not if you want to connect with people, anyway). The lack of duality is the single greatest advantage any non-profit has over a company if you're communicating well. The goal isn't to sell more or have a great quarterly statement; it's to improve the quality on an area of life.

Remember the story of Domino's Pizza and how they fearlessly adjusted their company in broad daylight? They told the story of their need to change, and then they made the changes. This is powerful because it is authentic. Your audience wants to hear a story that is consistently true and authentic.

That's why it's important to disclose negative events. I know it's not popular and I'm not advocating a public flogging of senior staff every time your plans or goals aren't reached. Convey the humanity of your organization; it's a positive selling point, not a negative one.

TAKE AWAYS

• Aim for three to five big campaigns per year.

• As the campaign ends, start acquisition push!

• Consistency, consistency, consistency.

• The event is not the end.

• Tease what's next to your audience; it starts your arc for the next campaign.

NEXT STEPS

• Look at your next year - How are you using story arcs to communicate?

• How are you rolling out the big guns for 4th Quarter efforts?

• What's the story of your organization practically communicated? Ask your team for input.

CHAPTER 4
RESPECTING YOUR AUDIENCE

"If a story is not about the hearer he will not listen. And here I make a rule - a great and interesting story is about everyone or it will not last."

- John Steinbeck

Story is a mainstream word that gets thrown around a lot, maybe too much. Some large agencies haven't figured out how to adjust their financial model to best aid their clients without largely relying on traditional mail. They operate on an old model of service and the whole communications world changed in the last five years. The decline of mail has been so rapid that I doubt any sector could have anticipated that kind of change.

Some agencies are adjusting but it's been a slow road. They're working very hard, they have some very smart people, and they are doing phenomenal work. However their model is set up on an outdated paradigm of print: "per piece."

So when it comes to the web, they have some serious issues because that model no longer applies. So they try to figure it out, they try to translate "per piece" costs to an hourly rate, and are largely going in circles. They may know your story but they don't know how to communicate in a mutually beneficial way in this new age of web.

Here's what I know with certainty: You have the best intentions to use the tools that you have at your disposal to the best of your ability. However, there is a disconnect that is happening and this disconnect is hurting you. The system that has worked for a long time with proven results is no longer in your best interest. Small organizations can deploy the same strategies as the large ones and usually create a system that has your best interest in mind without massive overhead.

Look at organizations like charity:water and Invisible Children. They haven't been around for too long so there's not a lot of legacy or previous way of doing things. They don't have to ease into a new age. They're in it. Their respective communications teams spend time engaging, impacting and creating events and campaigns that create a torrent of activity and donations.

	Behavior & Approach of Traditional Agencies vs The New System	

Current System (Agency)	New System (Boutique Agency)
Print is alive and well	Good/Strategic print is alive and well
Same message through all channels	Message that uses the strengths of each channel
Per Piece Pricing	Flat Rate Per Action
Slow Rollout on Tech	Easy Testing of New Tech
Technology Drives Donors to Print (a.k.a. The Mailing Address is most important to allow for another stamp)	Technology allows donors to make a choice on what channels they'd like to receive

Let's End the "People Alchemy," People

In the old model, the direct marketing manager would tweak and tweak and tweak to figure out the pinpointed demographics of the audience that they wanted.

"Pull a listing of people in Wichita that make over $70k that have given us a gift of over $200 sometime in the last 18 months. That's who we'll mail to."

That's great. It's specific. It's measurable. You can understand what's going on. Unfortunately, the temptation is to do some sort of "people alchemy" that obsesses over demographic message tweaking instead of focusing on what really matters... telling a great story.

Let's tell the BEST story we possibly can. It's important to be strategic with your message but it's also ABSOLUTELY CRUCIAL that your message is worth talking about.

Picture Your Future

We need a vision of the future. In other words, in 18 months from now if everything goes as planned, what does your organization look like? I want you to envision what happens if all of your pieces have come together. What's the ideal scenario?

Have you just existed? Are you just paying everybody and the lights are on? What kind of change did success make to the environment? What kind of impact did it make to the cause that you're fighting? Did it make a big difference? Was that difference in a specific place?

Massive change is not easy; it takes time and a clear vision. When I think of massive change in the face of adversity, I'm reminded of Jack Welch when he took over as CEO for General Electric in 1981. He's credited with the company mandate of "First, Second, Buy or Sell". Each of GE's businesses had to be either first or second in their field. If they weren't they'd have to buy a competitor to become at the top or they'd sell off and get out of it. It's amazing how much flack Welch took - from the Wall Street Journal to the New York Times - everyone just roasted him. He received such great names as "Jack the Hack" and "Neutron Jack" because outsiders didn't understand his restructuring. He was seeing the future of the world of business and knew his company needed to be ready.

As it turned out, this was a phenomenal strategy. General Electric got into new business and out of old ones, making such a big difference for their bottom line. The amazing part about it was <u>the way they defined their business.</u> They had to keep re-defining their markets to keep challenging their businesses to grow more and more.

So in your space, re-define things and get really specific. If you're fighting human trafficking, are you raising awareness in these local communities as well as raising money for global captures? Perhaps you've raised awareness in a school, or you've created a program. Get as specific as you can.

In Your Story, Your Audience = the <u>Who</u>

It makes sense to know your audience the best possible way you can and data is crucial. In this day and age, you need to be collecting information like email and cell phone numbers. It doesn't take much to do this and you should be doing it. You can set your website up to make sure that happens with some ease.

What we know MOST about your supporters and your audience is that they love you. Why? Because they are still hanging in there. They are with you in the good and the bad.

Take a quick survey of your audience and learn all you can. In moments you can create what Chris Brogan and Julien Smith refer to in their book, *Trust Agents,* a quick "listening post" to see what people are saying about your brand - and it's FREE!

Note: Social Media tools like Radiant 6 and Vocus offer fine services and they are top notch. There are others that can be nearly as effective like Hootsuite. They can help your org for $5 a month. Additional options like the search feature on Twitter (search.twitter. com) and Google.com are free.

Organizations will say to me: "Dan, we need Twitter and Facebook." And that may be true. But they aren't asking, "Where is our audience online?" This is a much more important question.

Is your audience on Twitter and Facebook? If you're trying to market to a bunch of high school kids, Twitter is probably not the place to connect with them. That doesn't mean that you don't want to talk to their parents, but that's a different audience!

So, who is your primary audience?

Who is your secondary audience?

I think it's a great idea for every non-profit to pick 2-3 audiences and decide:

"This is who we're going to target. Let's find out <u>everything</u> we can about them. Have they given before? Where are they coming from? Are they new to the donor file? How long have they been around? Do they give mostly gifts-in-kind? Are they cash givers? Do they give to special projects? Do they give in crisis? Where are they located? Do they connect with us on Facebook? Do they watch our videos?

Your audience is the <u>Who.</u> We want to know as much as we can about them.

They are smarter than most advertisers think! I love this piece by Hugh Macleod. [2]

---

2 http://gapingvoid.com/

IF YOU TALKED TO PEOPLE THE WAY ADVERTISING TALKED TO PEOPLE, THEY'D PUNCH YOU IN THE FACE.

©hugh

It's a great picture. It's terribly true.

Audiences are much smarter than you think and if you don't plan very well as an organization, some audiences will find your faulty assumptions very insulting. It's important to talk with your audience the way they want to be addressed. (See The Platinum Rule - http://bit.ly/rCyiEh) Remember you're the storyteller - engage with emotion and look to connect.

From Your Audience to Their Behavior

Next up is behavior, because this is directly connected with how we interact with our <u>Who.</u>

What is the action you want from your audience? Define it. I talk to so many organizations who say, "Dan, we need money!" My response is, "Okay, so you need donors. What else?"

Do you need awareness? Is there a massive push for acquisition of new donors or volunteers? What's the adage, "Failing to plan is planning to fail"? Define what success looks like and make sure your team knows it.

"We want a 10% increase in online giving."

"We want a 400% increase in online giving."

"We want to increase our volunteers by 30% over the next six months."

"We want to triple our Facebook likes and double our monthly Facebook interactions."

These are very specific goals and once defined, it's easier to create strategy and tactics around them.

From Their Behavior to a System

You've defined your audience, figured out their behavior, and now here's where systems go into place.

The question is: How often will you be communicating?

You're probably not surprised by this question, because it's old school and editorial calendars aren't going anywhere. It's much like direct mail. Online storytelling is very similar, the principals of good communication won't be changing. You will be communicating through some channels probably every month, or week, or day.

The danger occurs when your audience gets something in the mail from you too often and triggers the response, "My, you're spending a lot of money on me. Why are you spending money in this way?" This is a growing sentiment among Generation X and Generation Y donors.

But you can tweet me every day, multiple times a day, and you can post on Facebook. That doesn't cost you anything. It costs time.

Note: I'm not advocating throwing the baby out with the bathwater. If traditional media is decreasing by 20%, please don't automatically allocate those resources for digital. Look deeper into all that is happening and consider what the trends are industry-wide. A massive recent trend is that if your donors give online once and it was a pleasant experience, they will most likely give in that same way again.

Choose Your Medium Wisely

Next up is deciding how you'll be sending out your message. Often the channel has it's own culture and that will help determine the frequency, too.

Digital communication is its own animal and each "sandbox" or digital space like Facebook, Twitter, YouTube, has tools to connect your organization to great people. Please understand the type of person connected to your organization in each channel. They can differ widely depending on the rate of growth in each channel.

Facebook and Twitter have their own cultures. You have to be respectful of them and use them to help send signals to others that you "get it". If you're not involved with doing things like "Follow Friday" and "Music Monday" and "Charity Tuesday" on Twitter, you're missing out on the cultural tenants (specific to Twitter's network) that easily can help your organization take on a much more dynamic approach to storytelling.

Let it be known that there are actually people behind your organization's Twitter and Facebook accounts and, tell who they are - as long as they are willing. Adding humanity behind your brand is a good thing.

How is your promotion, campaign or offer going to look? How will you be cultivating this for your current donor and audience? How will they know they are valued? So they understand that you need them to keep the lights on?

How will acquisition look? Will you be asking people to promote this on your Facebook page, or to blog about it? Or are you going to do a Blog Tour? (A subject that is talked about on consecutive days on the blogs of different influencer's/people in your audience.)

Use your editorial calendar to schedule your Facebook updates, Twitter posts, YouTube releases, blog posts and email newsletters. Maybe spend a month on Facebook talking about X, while on Twitter you'll be focusing more on Y. You have two different mediums with two different ways of communicating. In just a few days you'll be weaving a multi-channel story. Add in some video and an email newsletter and you've got a campaign.

Facebook - A Tale of Two Possibilities

Facebook is a dichotomy. On one hand it can be the center of the digital world. 500 million users, everyone's connected. A huge amount of time on the site.

But it can also be limiting. Especially now that tribe members can unsubscribe from your updates. I would argue that if they want to unsubscribe, they aren't in your tribe and you don't have to worry about them. This is where slacktivism and motivations of guilt come in. This strategy works but only in the short term. Don't play that game.

Make sure your community is connected with you on Facebook and make sure you're not packaging the same exact content you're pushing out through Twitter. And definitely <u>DO NOT connect your Twitter updates to update your Facebook page.</u> If you do, what's the advantage of connecting with you through multiple channels? Diversify your content based on the channel and audience in that channel.

Facebook allows for greater connection so share more in that stream!

Feed the Puppy. Every Day.

Launching into social media is similar to getting a puppy. It's vitally important that you feed the puppy every day, in some way. Otherwise, you have a dead puppy on your hands. Nobody wants a dead puppy.

We've all been to those websites that haven't been updated since 2009. Nothing's happening. It makes you wonder, "What's going on with that organization? If their communication is down, are they doing anything? Do they still exist?"

Schedule your posts and remember to factor in when your audience is most likely listening. If you don't know, start testing.

Your Continuum of Communication

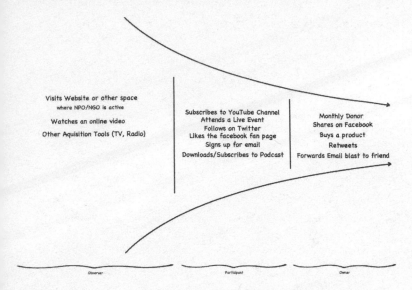

Visits Website or other space
where NPO/NGO is active

Watches an online video

Other Aquisition Tools (TV, Radio)

Subscribes to YouTube Channel
Attends a Live Event
Follows on Twitter
Likes the facebook fan page
Signs up for email
Downloads/Subscribes to Podcast

Monthly Donor
Shares on Facebook
Buys a product
Retweets
Forwards Email blast to friend

Observer

Participant

Owner

It's important to build a continuum of communication (or "a pathway of engagement.") As you'll see by the example, the continuum of communication is an easy way to flesh out the ways for people to get connected with you. As the audiences come in, they're going to check out your social media. It's all on their terms. They can look, they can peer in, they can see what's going on. They can sign up for email. They give you a little information, and you send something to their inbox.

Simply put, it is crucial that you don't abuse these modes. Sending a whole lot of email that's consistently just ASK ASK ASK, will not be received well (unless your audience loves it)! Tell them your story. Tell them how that money gets used. Tell them why it's important. The story makes all the difference in the world.

Create media pieces that move your audience closer and closer to the heart of your organization. Move them along the continuum from Observer to Participant to Owner. The biggest piece is that you've got to give them a reason. That reason might be an emotion, or a benefit, or one of a hundred reasons. This reason should be your <u>Why</u> or at least in the ballpark.

What's the first donation to an organization? A Volunteer's TIME

Moving forward on that continuum, suppose they like your messaging and now they are a volunteer. They decide, "I believe in what you're doing but I don't have much discretionary income." I'm sure you've seen this in your organization. Some audiences have more time than money right now so we're seeing them getting involved as volunteers.

The thing with volunteering is that it's like giving a stamp of approval. If they have a good experience in volunteering, they'll go ahead and make a donation to you, after the fact. But it's crucial to remember that in volunteering, they are already making a donation right off that bat with **their** time. Does your development department look at volunteers as making a contribution? Do they get thank you cards?

Your Volunteers are Your Storytelling Army

It's important that your volunteer department is cultivating this resource. Your volunteers are your storytelling army. They immediately talk about the experience. Is your volunteer department set up so that volunteers can get connected to where you are online? If they are spending time with your organization than they want to talk about it afterward. Help your biggest fans communicate what they did, how fun it was, and what a difference they made.

You can have a lot of fun setting up your brand on geo-location social tools such as Facebook Places/Gowalla, Foursquare and Yelp. Allow your volunteers to tell everyone that they are part of your story by checking into your event or writing a review about you.

Your volunteers have gone from being Observers to Participants. Give them the rewards and information they need to easily share your story with their networks. They are part of your tribe. They believe in your work and feel they are taking part in the mission. They are making a difference. They are fighting your antagonist with you arm-in-arm. They are part of your story and they know it. Use it to your advantage!

Help your tribe stand out from others. Do people get special volunteer t-shirts that can be purchased with a donation? Maybe there's a specific shirt <u>just</u> for people who volunteer often, because they make such a big difference. Who's not going to take photos about that and post them online?

Moving from Participant to Feeling Like an Owner

As you're thinking through your organization's plan for world domination please also define the holy grail of donors - the Monthly Recurring Donor. You know them. They pay online as a recurring donation and they "set it and forget it." This is the group that is really making a difference for your organization.

At this point they become an owner. An owner in your cause is one who is "all in". When they see your brand or hear about your work, they get "warm and fuzzies". They're impacting their network with your story, they're volunteering regularly and donating monthly. This is the promise land of donors!

They are as much on board with your organization as they can be without having a job there. You made a choice with your life in accepting a position at your organization but this crew is putting the gas in the tank. They're the reason work is being accomplished.

The best part about this audience is, if you can build it, you have such an incredible foundation to work from, because you know it's nearly guaranteed to convert. The Monthly Recurring Donor is where we should be leading our tribe.

Let's Talk KPIs

It's also very important that on the continuum of communication you're strategically monitoring your Key Performance Indicators (KPIs).

We can measure everything in the direct-mail marketing paradigm (How many pieces got mailed vs. How much came in?) but we can't measure if that appeal letter was glanced at, immediately ripped up, or read and then thrown away. In the digital world we can measure a lot and at a much faster rate. We can check real-time metrics to know immediately what happens when you launch a blog post or video.

KPIs must be set up to monitor things like website traffic, You Tube views, etc. What's the number of people getting connected to your Facebook page? Make sure that you're measuring more than just Facebook "likes," count interactions because that's the more important piece. We need to measure for impact <u>and</u> connection.

We also want to make sure that you're really leading your tribe online. There must be community growth. You want to give your audience what they need. This means that you must engage with them in some way on each channel.

This is an area where the so-called Social Media experts get into trouble. There has to be a conversion rate of some kind. It's not going to be an A + B = C scenario but there needs to be a connection between so many connection points in social media usually equals so much income.

Note: I'm a big fan of encouraging a tribe to donate but please don't be a one-trick pony. Social Media can be a source to lead to online donations but this road isn't always easily connected. I've found that with certain executive teams it's easier to put Social Media in the acquisition piece of the budget.

Show *(don't tell)* Me Your DNA

To communicate the best possible story for your organization it's important to show your DNA or personality in your communications. Organizations that use the digital space to mirror the reality of their day-to-day have the easiest time in the digital space. Why? Because they aren't creating extra work for themselves. Use your website to convey you, your office attitude and the work you do. This is definitely another case of simple-but-not-easy.

In 2008, I did some work with Union Rescue Mission (URM). They were the first to admit that their website needed some work. We spent time figuring out all of their great programming and what they were like. Asking questions like: What did the organization feel like? What are the adjectives I'd use to describe what I was seeing? What I felt? Prior to working with Union Rescue Mission, I was really unaware of what was happening in homeless services. It was incredible to see all of the programs that they had and it became evident quickly that there was a lot more of the story to tell than what was currently online.

Here's my summary on the site:

Facts about their website: There was a donate button or an appeal for financial contribution on the homepage no less than five times, three above the fold. Well-intentioned design but stiff and classically corporate.

The story their website was telling: Please donate to us. We have a lot of great programs but you probably won't find them on here.

The story that should be communicated:

Union Rescue Mission has life and death happen all around them on the tough streets of Skid Row. They're a safe harbor for over 1000 people per night because of their programs. They look to give their guests the life-changing resources they need to get back on their feet. With over 14,000 volunteers annually serving over 3,000 meals per day, they've got an army who care about their cause.

Next, I worked with a great designer, Kristin Myers. She listened to a whole bunch of the data I'd collected plus I told her the story about their programming and their services. She went to work to mirror this story. She played with some preconceived notions about homelessness in America and then used them as an opportunity to "poke the box" of many visitors' understanding. After taking a tour of the facilities at URM, one of the most common pieces of feed-back that they get is, "I had no idea you did all that!" I thought this would be a key piece for us to aim toward. Could we create a digital experience that would elicit that same kind of response?

What resulted was a great start in URM's embracing of new media. The website went on to win awards, the traffic tripled, more volunteers got connected and donations nearly doubled. Here's a picture of that site when we launched in October 2008:

Was this Jacques G., or omeone else?

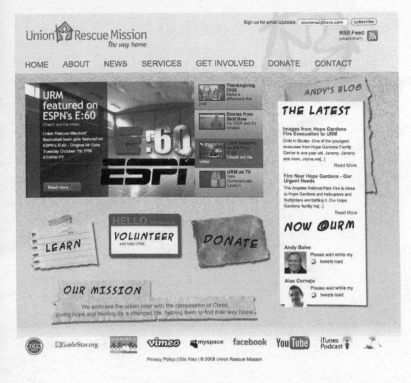

We realigned the site following year and we were able to build off the data that we received from analytics and as we got to know the tribe better, we could anticipate improvements.

Renown designer, Cameron Moll has a great article about redesign versus realigning and it's at the core of what we tried to do: http://bit.ly/sZY36h.

This site and the social media efforts that were made were highly successful for URM and resulted in a 75% increase in online revenue over the previous year.

Share It All

In the USA, Charity Navigator and EFCA monitor non-profits to make sure that they are fiscally responsible. But what if you went even further in your transparency with your audience? What if you talked about the good times AND the bad?

Remember that in a great story, not everything goes as planned.

If someone told you this story:

There once was a princess and she was from a great home. And she grew up and then she decided she wanted to go to a far away land. And she did! And everything there was great! And safe! And awesome! Then she met someone and they fell madly in love. And they lived happily ever after. The End.

That's a fine idea, but a terrible story. It doesn't make a lot of sense that there's no tension in that. Nobody's scared. There's nothing to conquer. There's no self-discovery.

It's so important in your organization to share the bad with the good. This is part of the task of telling a story that is true. Authenticity reigns.

Conversely, please don't tell the same consistent story of doom and gloom. Some organizations I see are only communicating "crisis! crisis! crisis!" It makes you wonder, "What ARE they doing?" Honestly, if an organization starts doing this, they're just signaling "We're not sure what's happening! We don't have great people!" That may not be true, but that's what they're communicating. The "crisis! crisis! crisis!" motif lets us know that this organization is having massive problems. This is not okay and tells a terrible story.

It's very important that you share good stories with the bad.

My favorite "bad story" shared online was Scott Harrison building/digging charity:water's 200th well, and it was streamed live. This was a big deal. charity:water in such a short time had made such a huge impact. So there they were, live, on location, and the excitement was palpable. Any minute they're going to hit water, and this village was now going to have access to clean water.

Live on the web, time was was ticking on, and on, and on. Harrison began visibly looking around, past the camera. His face was letting us know, "I'm not sure I can stall anymore."

This was supposed to be a BIG win for charity:water. It was supposed to be this giant climax and they never hit water.

He then spent that night, as anyone would, let down. He wrote this amazing blog post about how sometimes you don't win and the responses he received. It was so transparent, I thought you might want to see it here - http://huff.to/tgevUl

In the story sense, we felt that pain with him. Why? Because Harrison showed both his disappointment and real connection to the cause. We can empathize with the humanity of sometimes missing the mark.

In the story sense, we felt that pain with him.

Scott Harrison had the chance to share this downturn transparently to his audience. He was able to communicate:

1. We're human.
2. Sometimes things go wrong.

3. We really need help.

The best part? After Harrison wrote that blog post there was an outpouring of gifts and encouragement on and offline. One field engineer said, "Even with the best planning, scientific data and equipment, you can have a myriad of problems... thank you for sharing the challenges."

What a testament to charity:water and how they've cultivated their audience! It's also a testament to those who decided to get involved. Remember that this organization didn't try to manipulate this "bad story" in any way. Their tribe simply responded to the story that was unfolding.

Scott's story -> became the organization's story -> became the audience's story.

Transparency and trust are absolutely crucial for an organization to make this jump digitally. It won't happen overnight, but taking some steps on that road today is a great way to start.

TAKE AWAYS

- People are first, data second.

- Audiences are smarter than you think.

- The order of communication - Vision, Audience, Behavior, System

- Feed the social media puppy everyday

- Volunteers donate time first. It has value, just like monetary donation. Be sure to let them know they're appreciated.

- Share the highs and the lows.

NEXT STEPS

- Imagine the Vision for your organization.

- Determine your Audiences.

- Define the Behavior you need.

- Create a System to measure.

- Establish a KPI for every area where your organization is involved in. Then pick six to eight as the most crucial. Run these reports monthly.

- Audit your Website - What is it communication?

- How are you engaging your volunteers?

- Create a Continuum of Communication.

CHAPTER 5
BREAKING YOUR STORY DOWN BY CHANNEL

"A human being is a deciding being."

- Dr. Viktor Frankl

It's very important for any organization to be running on all cylinders. Running on all cylinders in the digital world means that you've got to be present in a lot of different social networks. These networks or sandboxes around the web allow you to interact with part of your audience that might not find you through traditional means. Your organization can now engage, cultivate, and build your audience virtually.

The great part of the social media world (a.k.a. the social "me") is that you get to be a lot more accessible. My personal network has developed by leaps and bounds just by being more accessible.

Work From Your Website Out

It all starts with a website. It's great to have all of these different channels, but if your website isn't too hot, you're in rough shape. The website is not the end game - community is. Gone are the days when you could put up a few pages like claiming a plot of land for your country. Your website has to be a living, breathing entity. You don't need a website, you need a hub of activity - a communication machine that never shuts off.

Start with a Website that Looks Good and is Highly Functional

Your website needs to:

1. Look good. It needs to be pleasing to the eye. If it's not, you're signaling that you don't care about how you communicate, and that you don't care about us as your audience. Make it as beautiful as you can manage. It doesn't need to be something that costs you six figures. I've seen some great websites for under $1,000.It should be highly interactive and functional.

2. It should be easy to navigate. In other words, the user experience should be a priority.

3. In conjunction with your website there is your blog. I can't tell you how many times I've been asked the question: Should I be blogging?

The answer is YES. You don't need a big consultant to set up a blog. You can set one up for free at Wordpress or Blogger or Tumblr or Posterous. There are so many options. You could literally be set up in minutes and then you're off to the races.

Some people get intimidated with the blog talk. What is a blog and how do I use it? In short, you need to have news updates. When something happens in your organization, a volunteer is outstanding, you received a grant, literally anything. Make sure that you're updating your entire audience with a blog/news update!

I think a great blog post includes a photo, some great copy, a call to action and it has some encouragement. Remember, you have a lot of tools in your storytelling arsenal. It doesn't all have to come back to "Make a Donation Today" in every post. If it does, you'll **alienate your audience.**

You could make a large investment in your website. Invest in the latest technology and have all the bells and whistles, but if you aren't creating consistently good content and telling your story - it doesn't matter. No one is going to visit more than once. The consistent content is the hook that gets your audiences to come back again and again.

I've heard of organizations that have paid over $100,000 for a website that did not have the option to consistently do news updates! Absurdity of absurdities! Don't let this be you.

Make Your Donate Button a One-Click Giving Machine.

One of the biggest (if not the biggest) crimes on the internet perpetrated by non-profits is frustrating the website visitor or user. I have visited many, many websites and checked out their homepages and I couldn't find the donate button. Or worse, I found five of them. What does this communicate to your visitor? How is it perceived? Turning your website into a billboard that says, "We Need Money!" doesn't make a positive impression.

A related, however regular, problem for many organizations is that after clicking to make a donation, I'm hit with too many options: Do you want to donate property? Do you want to donate monthly? This is the digital equivalent to back peddling when you're closing a sale. They want to donate, let them donate!! I understand that most organizations want to be as helpful as possible to their donors, so help them reach their goal. They clicked a donation button. They know where they want to go. It stands to reason that every click you ask your audience to make on the way to make a donation, you lose more and more of them. Don't alienate the people who want to give you money; make it easy for donors to give.

Do You Really Need that Microsite the Agency is Pitching?

Have you heard this pitch from the Ad Agency you're working with? "We'll do a mini-campaign and we'll get this microsite up and running." Remember, it is in the agency's best interest for you to pay for new sites. New sites means new billing. Microsites aren't all bad. But I haven't found them essential to the campaigns of any non-profit.

It's better for your overall site and brand if there's one place that I can come to to get connected to your mission. Have different branches of your site look and feel different, especially with new campaigns. Buy new domains and have them redirect to that part of the site. This communicates how savvy you are with your digital communication and eliminates the need for excessive billing for a nearly guaranteed low return on investment (ROI).

Keep your audience connected to your main website. Every time you do a microsite campaign, you're asking your audience to remember a new URL. Microsites can work for acquisition, but concentrate on building relationships and telling your story. Leave the gimmicks for when you've been wowing your audience for a while.

Social "Me" to Social "We"

As development directors and community developers it's important that we understand that one side the social web, in its purest sense, is all about "me" or about your consumers, donors and community. It's about how they're feeling. And this singular focus is to indulge every whim of selfishness.

The other side of the pendulum is that the social web is <u>very interested in the world in which we live.</u> On the social web, we get involved in the world's problems. We get involved either with (1) cash donations or (2) developing awareness. Doesn't that sound like music to your ears?

Enter the Orchestra

Your campaigns are established (Acts One, Two, and Three), and these are constantly being updated from the events and happenings of your organization. You're operating on all cylinders - your Continuum of Communication is flowing through multiple social media channels and your story is being told. When this happens, I think of it as The Orchestra. Remember, Facebook is different than Twitter, which is different than YouTube, which is different than LinkedIn.

All of these differences can be vilified because they aren't making it easy to have a one-size-fits-all plan or they can be championed for the way the can nuance your story and allow for different levels of communication. Sure, it can be overwhelming but you don't have to be in all of the sandboxes. Pick three to five social networks that you know your audience is a part of and get active in the space. Start tracking your KPI's and see who you're connecting with.

When it's done well, when it's all in sync and your departments are communicating in harmony, then The Orchestra of your Story will be a beautiful sound that will resonate out into the world.

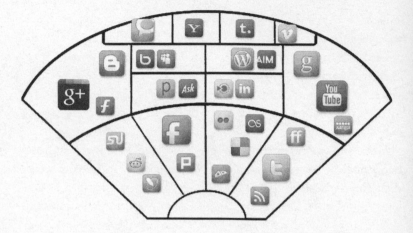

From Social Media to Email Marketing

Can you hear that? I can hear the echoes of your development department shouting (and whimpering), "Just send more emails and we'll see financial increase!"

Enter Email Marketing. Doesn't this sound very similar to our age-old Direct Marketing scenario?

Emailing more is not your problem. Cultivating a community is your problem. Your emails should tell your story just as the rest of your Continuum of Communication. How can you generate excitement by telling your Why? How can you invite your audience into your story to become participants?

Don't lose sleep trying to think up the best subject line for your emails - if you've got great stuff to share and a great story to tell - your emails will be opened. If you've really defined your audiences well, you could be destroying the national average for open emails.

From Email Marketing to New Media

Next a strong word about new media. Your organization should be creating something with video. You should set aside some money and bring in a real visual storyteller, a filmmaker who knows what you're trying to do, and knows how to communicate that in a visual form.

Ten years ago everyone said, "You gotta get a website." And what happened? So many organizations had a cousin or a friend or a son/daughter of a colleague set up their website. This same thing is now being applied in the film world: "Oh! I know a guy with a camera." Employing some guy with a camera is not helping your organization. I've found that the best filmmakers to collaborate with have big dreams and don't feel that client work is their endgame. They are pushing themselves and their company to be bigger, as a result, they are always learning. A posture of learning means that they'll have a careful eye on how to make your next film project.

Let me say this loud: You NEED a professional who knows what they are doing with video. Take a look at their work and see what they've done before. If their portfolio is filled with their homemade videos on You Tube, you haven't found a professional. Spend the money and make something remarkable. This is your story we're talking about!

Brevity is Nothing New

So many articles are hailing the new brevity of 140 characters, Twitter's means of sharing. It's an art form to communicate well in such a small space.

As legend tells it now, Ernest Hemingway was bet by his colleagues to write a short story with a beginning, a middle, and an end. Hemingway agreed and said he could do it in just six words. He then knocked them out with this gem:

"For sale, baby shoes, never used."

The story says they paid up. If Ernest Hemingway can do it with such power, I bet you can be very powerful with your words, too. You'll set up your organization for a big win with the social media in-crowd.

TAKE AWAYS

• Start with your website for look and feel, then move to social media and new media.

• Donating through your site should be easy. Make it one step!

• Microsites aren't really cutting it.

• When your social media is on all cylinders, you're in the Orchestra.

NEXT STEPS

• Make sure it's easy to donate online with your site. If not, fix it and fast!

• Look for your website to be much more than a land grab.

• Pick three to five social media sandboxes where you can be active.

CHAPTER 6
THE DEPARTMENT OF MEH

> "The opposite of love is not hate, it's indifference. The opposite of art is not ugliness, it's indifference. The opposite of faith is not heresy, it's indifference. And the opposite of life is not death, it's indifference."
>
> - Elie Wiesel

Two things spread on the web:

1. Things that are awesome.

2. Things that are awesomely terrible.

Most non-profits end up firmly in a middle area. I like to call this "The Department of Meh." This chapter is my clarion call to you: *This is your story.* Protect that baby and tell it the very best you can!

Think about your own appeals, think about the last several things you've sent out. Most organizations settle for an "OK" message in their campaigns…it's not really bad, it's not really good…it's just… "meh." You maybe shrug your shoulders at it. It's not compelling, but it's not horrid. It's meh.

Meh
1. Indifference; to be expressed when one simply does not care.

I know you tried hard. I hear so many organizations say, "Well, we're trying. We're doing the best we can." And that may be true. But that's also making excuses for the not-so-hot.

I know you can have an off month, or a season that's off… life happens. Constraints outside of work sometimes affect what you're doing. It's understandable. However, if your consistent message has been "just OK" for about the last year, I know exactly why your donations are dropping off.

When I begin talking to an organization, we dig in and assess the creative material they've created and released. There's a lot of looking at the floor. Very rarely is their pride in a recent mailing or campaign. So I'll ask:

"Would you open this? Does this make you feel good? What are your emotional triggers? How is it hitting you?"

I'll often get (very honest) answers like, "Mmm, no. No, not so much."

Get Mad

We need to rescue your content from The Department of Meh. No one can do it except you. You've got to get mad. You have to rally the troops and start thinking outside of the proverbial boxes that have surrounded you in the Department of Meh. Let's get some creativity flowing and shut it down.

The "Meh" is seriously killing your organization's ability to communicate.

Why is that? Perhaps you have a toxic scenario of people not being able to speak up. My guess would be that the tyranny of the urgent has got you down.

Let me just say, I understand. With everything in chaos and the economy tanking, you're doing the best you can with what you've got. I hear you. What if, instead of writing an appeal that HAD to happen once a month, you went much bigger and said, "We're going to drop having appeals happen so often, and instead we're going to make them so that they're BETTER and they are FEWER." (This may not be the best advice for your organization, only you'll know what you need to do!)

You have to take a stand to shut down the Department of Meh. Tell the most amazing, most engaging story you can.

Get Brave, Ask Your Audience

Really work with your audience. Talk with them! Ask them what they think. This is the best part about the social web. You don't need an official, expensive focus group - they're at your fingertips. You don't have to figure out the mailing and the survey with the results tabulation. You can make something as simple as a Facebook poll to ask how you're doing.

True, it takes a courageous organization to ask this vulnerable question. If an organization that I support asked me to tell them how they're doing, oh man! That's so much signaling. That says that they live in an abundance mentality, that they are very interested in being the best - how could I not help them?

Next, Ask Your Staff How You're Doing

Here's my encouragement: The next time your creative team gets together, ask some questions. Ask, "Is this the best we can do?" Do some research. See what other people are doing. Ask your team very honestly, "What do you think of this?"

Be prepared for an answer that isn't positive, especially if you don't feel like you're getting the best out of your appeals. Give people permission to speak their minds. Start your meeting with, "This may hurt, but I really want you to be honest." It may hurt to hear what your team says, but I assure you, your whole team will be better for it. That is a great thing, and this risk always pays off.

If you've given your team the ability to call out "the Meh" on the carpet, to truly call out the verbal shrug-of-the-shoulders, here's the wild paradox: I guarantee you that your team will be empowered to start creating better things. Now your closet creative genius that's been frustrated for the last six months and thinking about leaving will have an outlet to express.

Start thinking about how you're communicating in a story context. Ask how your audience is connecting and how you're building tension. Look especially at the places where your audiences haven't responded. As objectively as you can look for how you're communicating your story.

Look at every appeal and every campaign that you're communicating and ask, "How is this helping tell our story?" The days of expecting an automatic response on every campaign are over. Instead adjust your mindset to:

"I'm going to help tell the story of this organization and we're going to help solve the problem that we're fighting."

If you do this, you're going to be in a much better place emotionally, and you are going to begin to engage your audience for the first time. It'll even energize your team.

But, My Budget is Shrinking...

Now your budget may be even smaller than it was last year. You're doing more with less than you ever have before. The challenge now is to be creative, more creative than you've ever been. What are some ways to set up social signals to your donors and audience that you 1) need help and 2) have ways that they can get involved?

The crucial piece is implementation, not just creativity. Make sure your systems are in place. You've been creative on "What are our possibilities?" but a big effort needs to be the implementation.

Here's a couple quick options to engage your audience without spending a dime. (I'm sure you can think of some great additional options.)

- Take some small steps to test the waters.

- Ask your audience to fill out a five-question survey in your next email campaign. Use some thing free like Survey Monkey.

- Talk about that survey and the results on Facebook and Twitter.

- Highlight the individuals that speak up. Show your tribe the behavior you appreciate and you'll be engaging on a whole different level.

Remember you've got to walk before you can run and the more you engage, the more you'll learn. Create a great message and watch it spread. Develop a team of influencers or mavens to help spread your activity.

It is easier to mail more letters, but this is the path to great things.

TAKE AWAYS

• Two things spread on the web - The awesome and the awesomely terrible.

• Be bold in asking for a report card from staff and your audience.

• Resist the Meh.

NEXT STEPS

• Take a hard look at your communication.

• Ask your audience how they feel about connecting.

CHAPTER 7
YOU CAN DO IT

> "If you find yourself asking yourself (and your friends), 'Am I really a writer? Am I really an artist?' chances are you are. The counterfeit innovator is wildly self-confident. The real one is scared to death."
>
> - Steven Pressfield, _The War of Art:_ Break Through the Blocks & Win Your Inner Creative Battles

I've talked with many nonprofits and CEOs about a storydriven approach in theory and coached them through the practical and here's what I know - As long as you care about your organization and cause, you're the right person for the job.

My encouragement would be to take the action steps at the end of each chapter, have those tough conversations and augment your communication. You can do it. All the while building on the things that have worked in the past. Start small, get comfortable and then "unleash the hounds"!

This is the time to move forward, strike out and shake things up. There's plenty of resources and information on how to succeed. I've listed many of them in the back of this book.

I know it's a lot and it can be overwhelming. New approaches often are. If your communication is stagnant, a storied approach will be just the shot in the arm that you (and your team) need.

Please feel free to reach out to me and my team at Portnoy Media. We eat, sleep and breathe story concepts. Sign up for our email list (http://www.portnoymediagroup.com/email/) or reach out (http://www.portnoymediagroup.com/contact/) and let's talk about how we could work together on bringing a storied approach to your cause. We also put out information and resources on the blog; please help yourself.

The time for talk is over. Seth Godin says, "Real Artists, Ship" So grab your team and ship the best communication you can.

TAKE AWAYS

- You're the best person for this job! You can do it!

NEXT STEPS

- Roll up your sleeves, it's go time!

RESOURCES

On Story

The Hero with a Thousand Faces - Joseph Campbell

Story - Robert McKee - http://mckeestory.com/

Save the Cat - Blake Snyder - http://www.blakesnyder.com/

The Seven Basic Plots - Christopher Booker

On Communication

Switch - Chip Heath & Dan Heath -
http://www.heathbrothers.com/switch/

Resonate - Nancy Duarte - http://www.duarte.com/books

The Power of Pull - John Hagel III, John Seely Brown, and Lang
Davison

Tribes - Seth Godin - http://sethgodin.typepad.com/

Purple Cow - Seth Godin - http://www.sethgodin.com/purple/

On Ideas and Creativity

Start with Why - Simon Sinek - http://www.startwithwhy.com/

Making Ideas Happen - Scott Belsky -
http://the99percent.com/book

Where Good Ideas Come From - Steven Johnson

Ignore Everybody - Hugh MacLeod - http://gapingvoid.com/books/

Fascinate - Sally Hogshead - http://sallyhogshead.com/

The War of Art - Steven Pressfield -
http://www.stevenpressfield.com/the-war-of-art/

On Web Development

Don't Make Me Think - Steve Krug

Thank you for taking the time to read this book. Please send any feedback or questions to my inbox

Dan@PortnoyMediaGroup.com

Made in the USA
Middletown, DE
14 June 2015